THIS BOOK BELONGS TO

In Praise of
LOVE

JARROLD
PUBLISHING

IN PRAISE OF LOVE

LOVERS WALKING
Pellizza da Volpede 1868–1907

All love is sweet given or returned...
They who inspire it most are fortunate,
As I am now; but those who feel it most
are happier still.

Percy Bysshe Shelley

Love is more than gold or great riches.

John Lydgate

Duty makes us do things well,
but love makes us do them beautifully.

Reverend Philip Brooks

Love sought is good, but given unsought is better.

William Shakespeare

A person who has not loved
is like a candle that has not been lit.

Proverb

Love is the child of freedom, never that of domination.

Erich Fromm

To live without loving is not really to live.

Moliere

If you judge people, you have no time to love them.

Mother Teresa

*Love doesn't sit there like a stone,
it has to be made, like bread;
remade all the time, made new.*

Ursula K. Le Guin

*Tis better to love and be poor,
than be rich with an empty heart.*

Sir Lewis Morris

BY UNFREQUENTED WAYS
William Henry Gore 1880–1916

IN PRAISE OF LOVE

NAVAL MANOEUVRES
Edwin Roberts 1840–1917

All you need is love.

The Beatles

*L*ove must be fostered with soft words.

Ovid

Do you not see that you and I are as the branches of one tree?
    With your rejoicing comes my laughter,
With your sadness start my tears.
    Love, could life be otherwise with you and me?

Tzu Yeh

Grow old along with me!
    The best is yet to be.

Robert Browning

---

*T*hose who love deeply cannot age.

Arthur Wing Pinero

Drink to me only with thine eyes,
And I will pledge with mine;
Or leave a kiss but in the cup
And I'll not look for wine.

Ben Jonson

Love does not consist in gazing at each other,
but in looking together in the same direction.

Antoine de Saint-Exupéry

Faults are thicker when love is thin.

English saying

Love grants in a moment
what toil can hardly achieve in an age.

Johann Wolfgang von Goethe

THE LOVERS
AND THE SWANS
Gaston de Latouche
1854–1913

*People are always happy where there is love,
because their happiness is in themselves.*

Leo Tolstoy

---

*Love has a thousand varied
notes to move the human heart.*

George Crabbe

---

*We are all born for love,
it is the principle of existence
and its only end.*

Benjamin Disraeli

---

*Treasure the love you receive above all.
It will survive long after your gold and good health have vanished.*

Og Mandino

IN PRAISE OF LOVE

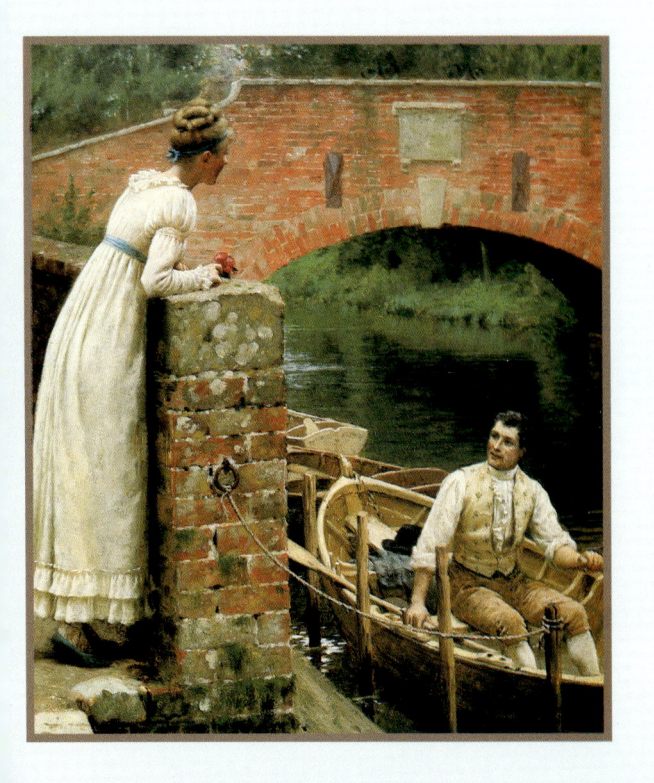

THE FOND FAREWELL
Edmund Blair Leighton 1853–1923

IN PRAISE OF LOVE

GATHER YE ROSEBUDS WHILE YE MAY
Theodore Blake Wirgman 1848–1925

Love must be within us before
it can be given.

I love thee – I love thee!
   'Tis all that I can say;
It is my vision in the night,
   My dreaming in the day.

Thomas Hood

❧

In a full heart there is room for everything,
and in an empty heart there is room for nothing.

Antonio Porchia

❧

A candle loses nothing of its
own light by lighting another.

❧

Love is something if you give away,
you end up having more.

Malvina Reynolds

❧

ℒove is a platform on which all ranks meet.

W. S. Gilbert

The entire sum of existence is the magic
of being needed by just one person.

Vi Putnam

Love is the one treasure that multiplies by division.
It is the one gift that grows bigger the more you take from it.
  It is the one business in which it pays to be an absolute spendthrift.
You can give it away, throw it away,
  empty your pockets, shake the basket,
Turn the glass upside down,
  and tomorrow you will have more than ever.

Love makes the world go round.

Popular song

IN PRAISE OF LOVE

A YOUNG WOMAN DRAWING A PORTRAIT
Abraham Solomon 1824–1862

The best portion of a good man's life is his little nameless,
unremembered acts of kindness and love.

William Wordsworth

IN PRAISE OF LOVE

Shall I compare thee to a summer's day?
Thou art more lovely and more temperate.

William Shakespeare

Love makes those young
whom age doth chill.
And whom he finds young keeps young still.

William Cartwright

The one thing we can never
get enough of is love.
And the one thing we never
give enough of is love.

Henry Miller

IN PRAISE OF LOVE

THE PRIDE OF DIJON
William John Hennesy 1839–1917

Love one another, but make not a bond of love;
Let it rather be a moving sea between the shores of your souls.

Kahil Gibran

Love, then, hath every bliss in store,
   'Tis friendship, and 'tis something more.
Each other every wish they give;
   Not to know love is not to live.

John Gay

Whatever you do... love those who love you.

Voltaire

'Tis better to have loved and lost than never to have loved at all.

Alfred, Lord Tennyson

IN PRAISE OF LOVE

LADY TENNYSON ON AFTON DOWNS
Valentine Cameron Prinsep 1838–1904

IN PRAISE OF LOVE

BY THE SEA
Povl Steffensen 1866–1923

What is irritating about love is
that it is a crime that requires an accomplice.

Charles Baudelaire

Of all forms of caution, caution in love
is perhaps the most fatal to true happiness.

Bertrand Russell

The course of true love never did run smooth.

William Shakespeare

There is only one kind of love,
but there are a thousand imitations.

Duc de la Rochefoucauld

Two human loves make one divine.

Elizabeth Barrett Browning

IN PRAISE OF LOVE

LOVE'S LETTER BOX
Arthur Hopkins 1848–1930

Time is...
    Too slow for those who wait,
Too swift for those who fear,
    Too long for those who grieve,
Too short for those who rejoice,
    But for those who love – Time is eternity.

Henry Van Dyke

IN PRAISE OF LOVE

HESPERUS
Joseph Noel Paton 1821–1901

*W*e have lived and loved together
Through many changing years;
We have shared each other's gladness,
And wept each other's tears.

Charles Jeffreys

A ROMANTIC PICNIC
Auguste Serrure 1825–1903

Two souls with but a single thought,
Two hearts that beat as one.

Von Munch Bellinghausen

To love and be loved is the greatest happiness of existence.

Sydney Smith

ALSO IN THIS SERIES

In Praise of Children
In Praise of Daughters
In Praise of Friends
In Praise of Grandmothers
In Praise of Happiness
In Praise of Life
In Praise of Mothers

First published in Great Britain in 1997 by
JARROLD PUBLISHING LTD
Whitefriars, Norwich NR3 1TR

Developed and produced by
FOUR SEASONS PUBLISHING LTD
1 Durrington Avenue, London SW20 8NT

Text research by *Pauline Barrett*
Designed in association with *The Bridgewater Book Company*
Edited by *David Notley*
Picture research by *Vanessa Fletcher*
Printed in Dubai

Copyright © 1997 Four Seasons Publishing Ltd

All rights reserved.

ISBN 0-7117-0958-0

ACKNOWLEDGEMENTS

Four Seasons Publishing Ltd would like to thank all those
who kindly gave permission to reproduce the words and visual
material in this book; copyright holders have been identified
where possible and we apologise for any inadvertent omissions.

We would particularly like to thank the following
for the use of pictures: *Bridgeman Art Library, e.t. archive,
Fine Art Photographic Library.*

Front Cover: THE ORCHARD, *Nelly Erichsen* fl. 1882–1897
Title Page: LOVERS EMBRACING IN A DOORWAY, *Rudolph Ernst* 1854–1920
Endpaper: THE LOVERS AND THE SWANS, *Gaston de Latouche* 1854–1913
Frontispiece: KING RENE'S HONEYMOON, *Dante Gabriel Rossetti* 1828–1882
Back Cover: THE EDGE OF THE WOODS, *Elizabeth Stanhope Forbes* 1859–1912